A LIFE GOD Rewards
for kids

BRUCE WILKINSON
& MACK THOMAS

ILLUSTRATED BY
DAN BRAWNER

MULTNOMAH KIDZ

SISTERS, OREGON

A LIFE GOD REWARDS FOR KIDS
published by Multnomah Publishers, Inc.
© 2002 by Exponential, Inc.

International Standard Book Number: 1-59052-095-5

Illustrations by Dan Brawner

Cover and interior design by Kirk DouPonce,
UDG|DesignWorks, Sisters, Oregon

Multnomah is a trademark of Multnomah Publishers, Inc.,
and is registered in the U.S. Patent and Trademark Office.

Printed in the United States of America

For information:
MULTNOMAH PUBLISHERS, INC.
POST OFFICE BOX 1720
SISTERS, OREGON 97759

02 03 04 05 06 07 08—10 9 8 7 6 5 4 3 2 1 0

CONTENTS

Chapter 1 — Stepping Out . . . . page 5

Chapter 2 — A Surprise . . . . page 13

Chapter 3 — Staying Longer . . . . page 21

Chapter 4 — Being Followed? . . . . page 29

Chapter 5 — Better and Better . . . . . . page 37

Chapter 6 — What Next? . . . . page 45

Chapter 7 — Way Up There . . . . page 53

Chapter 8 — Seeing Everything . . . . . . page 59

Chapter 9 — Seeing More Stars . . . . . . page 71

Chapter 10 — Now What? . . . . page 79

Dear Parents . . . . page 86

Scripture Verses Used in This Book . . . . page 90

Other Important Verses about Rewards . . page 92

God has so much to
show you about heaven...
and how you can make
living there better and better
forever and ever!
Come and read all about it!

CHAPTER ONE

Stepping Out

Kaleb and Emma had an ugly dog named Ruff Stuff. He had wild red hair that stuck out in every direction. He also had a stub-ugly nose that wrinkled when he barked.

Almost every day, Emma and Kaleb took Ruff Stuff for a walk around the block. They did it only because their mother told them to. They did not like doing it. Other kids who saw them would laugh at their ugly dog.

One summer Saturday morning, Kaleb and Emma were at home. They wanted to sit and watch TV all day long. But their mother came in and turned the TV off. "I have a job for you," she said. "Please take Ruff Stuff for a walk. And be back in time for lunch."

A LIFE GOD REWARDS *for Kids*

She also told them to take their little brother with them this time. They could pull him in the wagon. (Their brother's name was Brian, but Kaleb and Emma called him B Baby. Their mother *never* made him do jobs. She said he was too little. To Emma and Kaleb, this did not seem fair.)

They put Ruff Stuff on a leash. He wrinkled his nose and barked a happy bark. Then they stepped outside with B Baby.

It was already hot outside. There was no breeze.

"Let's get this over with," Kaleb said. He set B Baby down in the wagon. B Baby squealed a happy squeal.

"I'll pull the wagon," Kaleb told his sister. "You take Ruff Stuff." He threw the end of the leash on the ground beside her feet.

"No!" said Emma. She did not like their ugly dog. And she did not like Kaleb telling her what to do.

"Yes!" Kaleb ordered.

"No!" Emma said.

Suddenly they felt a cool little breeze. It seemed to circle right around them. It

ruffled Ruff Stuff's red hair. Then the
breeze quickly went away.

"Oh, forget it," Kaleb told Emma. He
picked up the leash.

Kaleb knew his sister was upset with
him. Yesterday, he had kicked her soccer
ball into the woods at the park and lost it.
And he never told her he was sorry.

Kaleb tied the dog's leash to the wagon. Then he started walking and pulling B Baby behind him. The wagon creaked and rattled and bumped, and B Baby smiled. He liked the noise, and he liked the bumps.

Ruff Stuff walked beside the wagon, sniffing with his wrinkly nose. He sniffed the curb. He sniffed someone's

SNIFF
SNIFF SNIFF

A LIFE GOD REWARDS *for Kids*

fence. He sniffed the ants that hurried across the sidewalk.

Emma ran ahead of them. Then she turned around and skipped backward. She tried not to step on any cracks in the sidewalk. (This is not easy to do when you skip backward.)

"I hate these walks," Kaleb said.

"Oh, stop complaining," Emma said as she skipped. "Maybe we'll run into something fun today."

Kaleb didn't answer. He didn't think anything good would happen on this walk. But he was wrong.

Why was
Brother Arlo mowing
the yard at the
Forget-It House?

CHAPTER TWO

A Surprise

Every time Emma and Kaleb walked around the block, they turned four different corners. And they passed seventeen houses. (They always counted them.)

But one house they never counted. No one lived there, maybe because it was too small. Plus, it needed painting. And the front porch had missing boards. And the grass in the yard was never cut. The children called this place the **Forget-It House.**

Today, they passed four houses and turned the first corner. They saw a little boy in his front yard. His name was J. T.

J. T. was standing under a tree. He was trying to reach a blue "Happy Birthday" balloon that was stuck in a tree branch. "Can you help me reach my balloon?" J. T. asked. "A breeze just came and blew it way up there."

Yesterday, J. T. had laughed at Ruff Stuff. He had also laughed at Kaleb and Emma. So Kaleb told his sister, "Just ignore him."

"Don't tell me what to do," Emma

said. Then she yelled at J. T., "Reach it
yourself, shorty!"

"Shhh!" Kaleb told her. "Emma,
you're so rude!"

"Am not!"

"Are too!"

They passed three more houses and turned another corner. Someone's big garbage can was at the curb. It was waiting to be emptied by the trash truck. But some of the garbage had spilled.

Emma hopped over the spill. "What a mess!" she said.

Ruff Stuff sniffed it. It did not smell good.

A LIFE GOD REWARDS *for Kids*

Kaleb pulled the wagon around the mess. He wondered if a breeze had blown it out of the garbage can.

They passed five more houses.

They turned another corner.

Then Ruff Stuff began barking and wagging his tail. Emma stopped skipping backward and turned around. Kaleb stopped pulling the wagon.

There in front of them was the Forget-It House. But it looked very different.

All the grass was cut. A man had mowed the yard, and now he was rolling his lawnmower back toward the house.

He wore a floppy fisherman's hat and a big smile.

Kaleb and Emma knew that smiling face. It belonged to Arlo Adams, their Sunday school teacher at church. Everybody liked him, and everybody called him Brother Arlo.

Why was Brother Arlo mowing the yard at the Forget-It House?

Emma and Kaleb just had to find out. After that, they could hurry home for lunch and more TV.

There was
a Bible lying open
on the edge of
the porch.

CHAPTER THREE

Staying Longer

Hello, Emma and Kaleb," Brother Arlo called out across the yard. Then he laughed. "If you came to help me cut grass, you're too late! But you can help me paint. Come on over!"

His face was shiny with sweat. His hat had fishhooks stuck in it, and the sunshine made the fishhooks sparkle.

Kaleb pulled the wagon off the sidewalk and toward the house. Emma and Ruff Stuff followed him across the fresh-cut grass.

The front porch had new boards in it to cover the holes. Paint buckets and brushes were sitting nearby. A ladder was leaning against the house. And there was a Bible lying open on the edge of the porch.

Kaleb parked B Baby's wagon beside the bottom porch step. Then he untied the dog's leash. Ruff Stuff sniffed the new boards and the paintbrushes.

Brother Arlo scratched Ruff Stuff behind his ears. "This dog is almost as ugly as I am," he said.

Then Brother Arlo lifted B Baby out of the wagon. He took a shiny silver case out of his pocket and let B Baby hold it. "Here you go, buddy," he said. Inside the case was a tape measure that pulled out and then snapped back with a *shhhk* when you let it go. Brother Arlo showed B Baby how it worked. B Baby kept pulling it out and letting it snap back. He liked the *shhhk* noise it made.

Brother Arlo picked up a paint bucket and started shaking it.

"What are you doing?" Emma asked.

"Mixing up the paint." Brother Arlo's nose wrinkled. It always wrinkled when he smiled.

"I know you're mixing paint," Emma said. "But why are you doing it here? Why are you fixing up this old place?"

Just then the screen door creaked opened. A bent-over woman with white hair walked out on the porch with slow little steps. "Who are your friends, Brother Arlo?" she asked. A smile showed through all her wrinkles.

"Miss Maggie, these are my Sunday school students, Kaleb and Emma, with their baby brother," Arlo said. "Children, this is Miss Maggie Parker. She was sick for a long time. But now she's doing better, and she has just moved into her new house."

"Good morning to you all," Miss Maggie said. "And what a warm morning it is! Can I offer you some lemonade?"

That sounded good to Kaleb and Emma. But they did not want to say yes. Miss Maggie moved so slowly. It would take her a long time to bring them anything. They might never get home today to watch TV.

Brother Arlo quickly spoke up. "Lemonade would be just *wonderful*, Miss Maggie! Yes indeed, we would *all* like some. Right, children?"

"Yes, please," Kaleb said.

"Yes, please," Emma said with a shrug.

"If Jesus rewards someone for giving away a cup of cold water, just think what He will do for someone who gives away a cup of icy lemonade!"

Being Followed?

Miss Maggie walked with slow little steps back inside her house.

Brother Arlo picked up two more paint buckets. "Would you like to help me shake them up?" he asked Kaleb and Emma.

The buckets were heavy. Emma and Kaleb kept shaking them back and forth, upside down and right side up.

A cool little breeze blew across the porch. It turned the pages in the open Bible that was lying there.

B Baby stayed busy with the tape measure. He seemed to be measuring every inch of the wagon and the bottom porch step. Pull. *Shhhk.* Pull. *Shhhk.* Pull. *Shhhk.*

"Miss Maggie had to stay in a hospital bed for a long, long time," Brother Arlo said. "But now she's up and going, and she wants to do all she can to help other people. So don't worry about her bringing us lemonade. She's so glad to do it. And she knows Jesus will reward her for it."

"What do you mean?" Kaleb asked.

Brother Arlo plopped his bucket on the ground. His nose was wrinkled, and his eyes were wide and twinkly. "Why, Kaleb! Don't you *remember?* We talked about it in Sunday school!"

He leaned over to look at his Bible. "Listen to what Jesus promised," he said. He read these words out loud:

> "Suppose someone gives you a
> cup of water in my name
> because you belong to me.
> That one will certainly not go
> without a reward."

"Did you hear that? If Jesus rewards someone for giving away a cup of cold water, just think what He will do for someone who gives away a cup of icy lemonade!"

Brother Arlo took a screwdriver from his back pocket and used it to pry the lids off the buckets. And he said, "While Miss Maggie earns a reward by bringing

A LIFE GOD REWARDS *for Kids*

us lemonade, you can earn rewards by helping me fix up her house. She's too old and slow to do this work herself. And she's too poor to pay someone else to do it. I'm glad I can do it for her. Would you like to help?"

They weren't sure what Brother Arlo meant by "rewards." Maybe he would pay them for helping him.

"Sure," said Kaleb.

"Why not?" said Emma.

Brother Arlo handed a brush and an open bucket to each of them. "Not a drop on your clothes, okay?" They nodded.

They started spreading the bright white paint onto the dirty gray front of the little house. What a difference it made!

Now and then the little breeze would blow once more across the porch. Kaleb and Emma saw the Bible's pages turning.

"Is that breeze following us?" Emma asked her brother.

"Maybe so," Kaleb answered.

"Someone is building
a huge, awesome place
for us! He went there to
get it all ready!"

CHAPTER 5

Better and Better

Most of the house front was bright with new paint when the screen door creaked again and Miss Maggie came out. She held a tray with five paper cups of lemonade. There was also a bowl of water on the tray.

"The water is for your dog," Miss Maggie said. "He looks thirsty."

Brother Arlo stepped down from the ladder to help Miss Maggie serve the lemonade. He set the water bowl on the ground for Ruff Stuff. He also brought out a rocking chair from the house to the porch, so Miss Maggie could sit outside with them.

He sat on the bottom porch step and said, "Ten-minute break for everyone!" He drank his lemonade in one gulp. Then he helped B Baby drink from his cup without spilling it.

Emma and Kaleb sat down on the top step behind Brother Arlo.

They all looked out across the yard. Over the fresh-cut grass, white butterflies danced in the air.

A LIFE GOD REWARDS *for Kids*

Emma sipped her lemonade and looked over her shoulder at the tiny house behind her. "Your new home is not very big, Miss Maggie."

Kaleb frowned at his sister to signal that she was being rude. But Emma ignored him.

Miss Maggie smiled. "Oh, it isn't home for very long," she said. "Only until I move into my super big house! It's being built for me right now."

Emma looked around her. "Where will your super big house be?" she asked.

Brother Arlo's nose wrinkled again. "Don't you *remember?*" he said. "Someone is building a huge, awesome place for us! He went there to get it all ready!"

Now Emma remembered. "Oh, yeah…heaven."

Brother Arlo jumped up. "That's right! *Heaven!*" He clapped his hands together. "*Yes!*" he shouted. He took off his floppy hat and threw it spinning into the air. The fishhooks on it sparkled.

Ruff Stuff barked a happy bark. And B Baby squealed a happy squeal.

"Oh, I get so excited!" Brother Arlo said. He leaned over again to read from his Bible. With his hat off, his wild red hair was sticking up in every direction. "Listen again to what Jesus promised," he said.

> "There are many rooms in my Father's house.... I am going there to prepare a place for you.... I will come back. And I will take you to be with me. Then you will also be where I am."

"So Jesus Himself is getting everything ready for us, until the time comes to take us there to be with Him! Heaven will be so great, Emma! Heaven will be so exciting, Kaleb! Isn't that right, Miss Maggie?"

Miss Maggie smiled as she rocked in her chair. "In heaven, we will always be with the Lord," she said. "We will always be doing fun things with Him. Living there will be so wonderful!"

She stopped rocking and leaned forward. She looked back and forth from Emma to Kaleb. "And by helping Arlo today, you're making it even *more* wonderful."

The children looked at each other.

"How?" Emma said.

"What do you mean, Miss Maggie?" Kaleb asked.

"Kaleb! Emma! Don't you *remember?*" Brother Arlo said again. "Don't you remember how you can make living in heaven better and better forever and ever?"

Kaleb and Emma shook their heads.

Then Ruff Stuff growled a little. And B Baby whined a little.

"When Jesus died on that cross, He was taking our place. He was being punished for us—for all the wrong things we do."

CHAPTER SIX

What Next?

Brother Arlo picked up B Baby from beside the bottom step. He carried him up to Miss Maggie so she could rock him in her lap.

Then he said to Kaleb and Emma, "I guess I need to remind you of some things we talked about in Sunday school."

"Maybe we weren't paying attention that day," Kaleb said.

"Yeah," said Emma. "Maybe we were talking with our friends instead of listening."

"I'm glad you like talking with your friends," Brother Arlo told them. "But isn't it more important to find out how to make living in heaven better and better forever and ever?"

"I guess so," Emma said.

"For sure," said Kaleb. "So what did we miss?"

"Let's find out," Brother Arlo said. "Let's go back to the beginning. And let me ask a question. Do you know why you can go to heaven?"

Emma and Kaleb nodded. That was something they *did* remember.

"There was a cross," Emma said. "A big wooden cross. And Jesus was nailed to it and He died."

"He was being punished," Kaleb added. "But Jesus had never done anything wrong, because He is the perfect Son of God. When Jesus died on that cross, He was taking our place. He was being punished for us—for all the wrong things we do."

As Kaleb and Emma spoke these words, what Jesus did seemed more amazing than ever. God loved them so much!

A LIFE GOD REWARDS *for Kids*

"When we were little," Emma said, "we prayed and told God that we believe in Jesus. We invited Jesus into our hearts, and He came in. And that's why we can go to God's heaven. Isn't that right?"

"Absolutely," Brother Arlo said. "That's exactly what God promises. That's why I'm so happy that Jesus died for us." Brother Arlo leaned back and looked up into the sky. It was very blue today. There were just a few clouds, and they seemed especially white, with soft silver edges. "Thank You, Jesus, for giving us heaven," Brother Arlo said.

A little breeze blew again and fluttered through the Bible's pages. And out across the yard, the white butterflies danced.

Then Miss Maggie said, "Now I have a question for you, Kaleb and Emma. After we reach heaven, what will happen next? Do you know?"

"No," Emma said.

"I'm not sure," Kaleb said.

"Well," said Miss Maggie as she slowly rocked, "one super important thing that will happen is this: In heaven, each one of us will stand before—"

A LIFE GOD REWARDS *for Kids*

She stopped rocking again. "Oh," she said, "let's do this right. Brother Arlo, why don't you help them imagine it?"

"I'll try," Brother Arlo said. He looked at Kaleb and Emma. "Did you bring your imaginations with you?"

Kaleb nodded. "I think mine's here somewhere."

And Emma said, "I always have mine!"

"Then let's fly!" Brother Arlo said.

"In fact, we can hear
the angels singing now.
Their music is loud,
and it's beautiful."

CHAPTER SEVEN

Way Up There

Brother Arlo walked back and forth in front of the porch. He kept staring into the sky.

He raised his arm and pointed straight up. "What do you see way up there?" he said.

"Clouds," Kaleb answered.

"White puffy clouds," Emma said. "With shiny silver edges."

"Yes indeed," Brother Arlo said. "And now, imagine that we're flying up through those clouds. We're flying far beyond their silver edges, higher and higher.

"And we're moving into the future. We're moving toward heaven. In fact, we can hear the angels singing now. Their music is loud, and it's beautiful. In fact, everything sounds beautiful up here. And everything looks beautiful too. We're seeing stars and galaxies up close. It's all so incredible.

"And now we're coming to a huge throne. There are rainbows all around it. And there's a deep ocean stretching out before it that's as clear and still as glass.

This throne is the throne of a mighty King. It's the place where He sits and rules over everything and decides everything. Can you imagine that throne? Can you see it?"

"Yes," answered Emma and Kaleb.

"And who do you think that mighty King is?"

"Jesus," they said.

"Jesus indeed," Brother Arlo said. "King Jesus." Then Brother Arlo bent down close to them and whispered, "And the Bible says that each of us will step close to that throne. We'll be standing right there, right out in the open, before the great and mighty King. Before the awesome King, the only King of kings."

Brother Arlo's whisper became even more hushed. "And what do you think

A LIFE GOD REWARDS *for Kids*

happens next? Why does the awesome King Jesus have you there? What will He say? What will He do?"

Emma and Kaleb shook their heads. They stayed quiet. And B Baby was quiet. And Ruff Stuff was quiet.

Brother Arlo stood on his feet again. His voice boomed out: "Oh, Emma, it's so amazing! Oh, Kaleb, it's so spectacular!" He stared into the clouds again.

Emma looked up too. "What is it, Brother Arlo?"

"Please tell us!" Kaleb said.

"Jesus will reward us!
And not only that, but He will
show us exactly what He's
rewarding us for!"

CHAPTER EIGHT

Seeing Everything

What happens next," said Brother Arlo, "is that Jesus will *reward* us! And not only that, but He will show us exactly what He's rewarding us for!"

"How?" Kaleb asked.

"By judging everything we did in our life on earth. 'Judging' means that He measures it, sort of like a tape measure does. But Jesus doesn't measure how long something is. He measures how *good* it is."

Brother Arlo read from the Bible again:

> *We must all stand in front of Christ to be judged.*

A LIFE GOD REWARDS *for Kids*

"God's Good Book is telling us that we will all get measured like that. And He says that we'll be judged for absolutely everything we do while we are in our bodies—while we live on this earth. Jesus will look at every single thing we did in our life on this earth as His children. Everything! And He will let us see it all while He's judging it."

"He will?" said Kaleb.

"I didn't know that," said Emma.

"But it's true," Miss Maggie said. They turned toward her. She was rocking gently, and B Baby was resting peacefully in her lap. "The Bible tells us that when we stand before Jesus, an amazing fire will be there. Everything we have done in our life will be put through this fire. The fire will help us see it all."

Brother Arlo turned to another page in the Bible. "Here's what Miss Maggie is talking about," he said. He showed the page to Kaleb. Kaleb found the words and read them out loud:

> *Each person's work will be shown for what it is. On judgment day it will be brought to light. It will be put*

through fire. The fire will test

how good everyone's work is.

"But what does that mean?" Kaleb
asked. "What is this fire?"

"It's a testing fire," Miss Maggie
answered. "But it won't touch you; it will
only touch the things that you did in your
life. It will burn up all the worthless
things you did—like just sitting and
watching TV all day. But all the good
things you did will not burn up. The good
things will come through the fire just
fine. They will shine bright like gold or
silver or diamonds.

"On that same page there, the Bible says that living on this earth is like building a house. When we do worthless things, it's like building our house with straw. And whenever fire comes, a straw house burns to ashes!

"But when we do good things, it's like building our house with gold or silver or diamonds. And a house made of gold or silver or diamonds will never burn.

"And of course, no matter how many worthless things there are in our life, God will never send us out of heaven. Jesus made sure of that!"

"Okay," Emma said, "so the good things we do will come through the testing fire just fine. I understand that. But how do we make living in heaven better and better?"

"That's what I want to know too," Kaleb said.

"God's Good Book will show you," Miss Maggie said. "Look on that same page. What does it say about reward?"

Kaleb found these words:

The Lord will give each of us a reward for our work.

And these words too:

If the building doesn't burn up,
God will give the builder a
reward for his work.

"Does that mean," Kaleb asked, "that
God will give us a reward for everything
we do that doesn't get burned up in the
testing fire?"

EXACTLY!

"Exactly," said Miss Maggie. "God has promised! We will be rewarded for all the good things we did for God, and for all the times we worked hard for Him. He will reward us for everything we did for Him."

"Everything?" Emma asked.

"Everything!" said Miss Maggie.

"And let me tell you why," Brother Arlo said. "It's all because of how *good* God is!" he said. "He's so fair! He's so generous! He's so giving!"

He read from the Bible again:

God is fair. He will not forget what you have done.

"God doesn't forget anything!"
Brother Arlo said. "And listen to what
Jesus tells us on the very last page of
the Bible:

"Look! I am coming soon!
I bring my rewards with me.
I will reward each of you for
what you have done."

"Just imagine it," Brother Arlo said.
"When we see Jesus at last, He will have
His rewards with Him. Incredible
rewards! Crowns and thrones and
mountains and stars and galaxies—and

so much more than we could ever imagine."

The children looked up. High in the sky, the clouds were moving slowly with the wind.

"And I wonder," Brother Arlo said to Kaleb and Emma, "how many of those rewards will be for *you.*"

69

"If you're doing good things for God every day, you'll receive more rewards from Jesus. And that will make living in heaven better and better forever and ever."

CHAPTER NINE

Seeing More Stars

That's what Kaleb and Emma were wondering too: How many rewards would Jesus have for them?

Miss Maggie and Brother Arlo were right. Those verses in the Bible about rewards were amazing and wonderful.

"When I go fishing at the lake," Brother Arlo said, "I like to go in the early evening, when the fish are hungry for their dinner. I sit on the shore and watch the sunset fade away, and the stars come out. Just a few stars are shining at first, and then more and more and more. Soon the whole sky is full of shining stars. I love to look up and see so many.

"But what if I stayed here and tried to look at the stars through that little keyhole in Miss Maggie's front door? I could never see the full picture. I could never understand how big and beautiful the night sky is.

"When we don't understand what the Bible says about rewards, it's like looking at the stars through a keyhole. God wants us to know all about them.

He wants us to look forward to rewards. This will help us to keep working hard for Him.

"If you're doing good things for God every day, you'll receive more rewards from Jesus. And that will make living in heaven better and better forever and ever."

Kaleb asked, "So what are the good things we should do?"

"God will show you," said Brother Arlo. "He will show you all kinds of good things you can do for Him each day. God will show you as you read His Good Book. As you pray to Him throughout the day, He will show you people you can help and people you can love.

"God has promised to help us. In fact, let's pray right now and ask for His help."

Brother Arlo looked up at the sky, "Our Father," he said, "thank You for the wonderful home You're getting ready for us in heaven. And now, show us today and

ARF!

A LIFE GOD REWARDS *for Kids*

every day exactly what You want for us, so we can do the things that make You happy!"

Ruff Stuff barked, and Brother Arlo laughed. "That sounded like an amen to me," he said. He reached over and scratched the dog's head. "And now it must be time to get back to work."

"Oh, but there's no rush on the house," said Miss Maggie. "Why don't we have lunch now? I'll make something, and we can all keep talking while we eat."

"Oh—is it that late already?" Emma asked.

"That means we need to hurry home," Kaleb said. "Our mother told us to be back by lunchtime."

"You better run along then," Brother Arlo said. "I can finish the painting. You've helped a great deal already."

Kaleb lifted B Baby from Miss Maggie's lap and put him into the wagon. He started to tie the dog's leash to the wagon, but Emma smiled and said, "I can take Ruff Stuff."

"Please come back to see me," Miss Maggie said.

"We would like to," said Emma.

"Yes," Kaleb agreed. "We want to keep helping Brother Arlo fix up your home here. We used to call this the Forget-It House. But we won't forget it anymore."

"You're welcome to help me anytime," Brother Arlo said.

Emma and Kaleb said good-bye and walked across the grass and onto the sidewalk. They decided to go home the same way they had come.

While they walked, they both were wondering: What else could they do today to make God happy and gain more rewards in heaven?

"What should
we do now to make
God happy?"

CHAPTER TEN

Now What?

A gentle breeze was blowing from behind Kaleb and Emma. It almost seemed to be pushing them along.

They turned the corner.

"I'm glad that we took this walk today," Kaleb said. "And that Brother Arlo and Miss Maggie showed us those things from the Bible."

"And that we could earn some rewards by helping with her house," Emma said. "But what should we do now to make God happy?"

"God will show us," Kaleb said. "That's what Brother Arlo told us."

They passed five houses. They came to the spilled garbage.

"Why don't we pick this up?" Kaleb said.

"Good idea," said Emma. It took only a minute to clean up the mess.

They turned another corner and passed three houses. In the front yard of the fourth house, they saw J. T.'s birthday balloon still caught in the tree.

"Let's get it down for him," Emma suggested.

"Good idea," said Kaleb. He pulled
the wagon under the tree. Emma held
B Baby while Kaleb turned the wagon
upside down and stood on it to reach the
balloon. Then they rang the doorbell. J. T.
answered it.

"I'm sorry I called you shorty,"

Emma told him. "Here's your balloon. And happy birthday!"

J. T.'s eyes opened wide with wonder.

Kaleb said, "Maybe you could come with us sometime when we walk our dog?"

J. T. looked at Ruff Stuff. Then he nodded. "Your dog looks funny," he said. "But I like him."

Ruff Stuff barked a happy bark.

The children told J. T. good-bye and went on their way. The breeze was still behind them. The wagon creaked and rattled and bumped, and B Baby squealed.

They turned another corner.

Ruff Stuff started sniffing another fence. Kaleb looked over at his sister as she pulled on the leash.

"Thanks for taking Ruff Stuff," Kaleb told her. "And I'm sorry I lost your soccer ball yesterday. The next time we go to the park, I'll try to find it for you."

"Thanks," Emma said.

They passed three more houses.

"We're home," Kaleb said. He reached down to lift B Baby out of the wagon.

He held his brother in his arms and pointed to the sky. "Look, Brian," he said.

"Look at the clouds. Way up there, we have a super big home waiting for us."

Emma reached down to undo Ruff Stuff's leash, and gave him a hug. Then she stood close beside her two brothers. She looked up at the sky with them and said, "And we can make living there better and better..."

"...forever and ever," Kaleb added. "Let's do it today."

"And never stop," said Emma.

And Ruff Stuff barked. And B Baby squealed.

—

Dear Parents

You can help your child discover the good things God wants us to do each day. God has a special plan for each of us! And He promises to reward us for every good thing we do for Him: "You know that the Lord will give you a reward. He will give to each of you in keeping with the good you do" (Ephesians 6:8).

Here are special ways to help your child in this:

◆ Keep showing your child how to pray throughout the day, asking for God's guidance and help. Model this for your child as often as you can by praying aloud. And talk about how God answers these prayers for you.

God wants to be very actively and personally involved, hour by hour, in our lives!

◆ Read the Bible together. When you come to commands that God has for us in Scripture, mention that God will reward us when we obey these commands. Talk about how we show our love to God by obeying His Word.

◆ Talk especially about being alert to the needs of other people. Help your child see that all around us are people we can help and love and encourage, all for the sake of Christ.

◆ Look for practical things you and your child can do together to help someone.

When you make the most of those opportunities, talk afterward about how God made this need known to you, and how you can be open to seeing similar needs in the future.

◆ Discuss how we show our love for God by loving other people. Talk about helping classmates at school, friends at church, neighbors, relatives, and people you encounter as you shop or travel. Talk as well about helping people your child doesn't like. Help your child begin to realize that every human being is someone we can serve for Jesus' sake, and that He will reward us.

What exactly can you and your child do to help others? There are so many things! What does your child especially enjoy doing? What are your child's special abilities and skills? These might well be ways that God wants your child to be actively involved in serving others.

◆ Talk with your child about how it's easy to waste time doing things that don't honor God, and that don't bring true and lasting benefit to other people or to ourselves. Learn together to be sensitive to these distractions, and to eliminate them.

And don't forget:
For all these ways that you help your child, God will reward you as well!

SCRIPTURE VERSES USED IN THIS BOOK

Page 31 —

"Suppose someone gives you a cup of water in my name because you belong to me. That one will certainly not go without a reward."

MARK 9:41

Page 41 —

"There are many rooms in my Father's house.... I am going there to prepare a place for you.... I will come back. And I will take you to be with me. Then you will also be where I am."

JOHN 14:2–3

Page 60 —
We must all stand in front of Christ to be judged....

2 CORINTHIANS 5:10

Page 61 —
...while we are in our bodies. Then all of us will receive what we are supposed to get.

2 CORINTHIANS 5:10

Pages 62–63 —
Each person's work will be shown for what it is.
On judgment day it will be brought to light. It
will be put through fire. The fire will test how
good everyone's work is.

1 CORINTHIANS 3:13

Pages 65–66 —
The Lord will give each of us a reward for our
work.... If the building doesn't burn up, God will
give the builder a reward for his work.

1 CORINTHIANS 3:8, 14

Page 67 —
God is fair. He will not forget what you have
done.

HEBREWS 6:10

Page 68 —
"Look! I am coming soon! I bring my rewards
with me. I will reward each of you for what you
have done."

REVELATION 22:12

SOME OTHER IMPORTANT VERSES
ABOUT GOD'S REWARDS:

Psalm 62:12

Isaiah 40:10

Isaiah 62:11

Matthew 6:19–20

Matthew 10:42

Matthew 16:27

Luke 6:22–23

Luke 6:35

Romans 14:10–12

1 Corinthians 4:5

Galatians 6:9

Ephesians 6:8

COLOSSIANS 3:1–2

COLOSSIANS 3:24

HEBREWS 11:6

2 JOHN 1:8

Begin an Eternal Adventure

A LIFE GOD REWARDS GUYS ONLY
Speaks specifically to developing young men, helping them live their lives to make a difference forever.
ISBN 1-59052-096-3

A LIFE GOD REWARDS GUYS 90-DAY CHALLENGE
More than just a devotional, this is a personalized challenge to find out how to please God in everything you do today.
ISBN 1-59052-098-X

A LIFE GOD REWARDS GIRLS ONLY
A revolutionary message presented in a captivating package for girls 9–12 as they begin to form their feminine identity.
ISBN 1-59052-097-1

A LIFE GOD REWARDS GIRLS 90-DAY CHALLENGE
More than just a devotional, this is a personalized challenge to find out how to please God in everything you do today.
ISBN 1-59052-099-8